Th Jefferson

Writer, Leader, President

Darleen Ramos

Boston, Massachusetts
Chandler, Arizona
Glenview, Illinois
Upper Saddle River, New Jersey

Illustrations
3, 4 Bradley Clark.

Photographs
Every effort has been made to secure permission and provide appropriate credit for photographic material.
The publisher deeply regrets any omission and pledges to correct errors called to its attention in subsequent editions.

Unless otherwise acknowledged, all photographs are the property of Pearson Education, Inc.

Photo locators denoted as follows: Top (T), Center (C), Bottom (B), Left (L), Right (R), Background (Bkgd)

Opener: Library of Congress; 1 Library of Congress; 2 Medioimages/Photodisc/Thinkstock; 5 Photos to Go/Photolibrary; 6 Thinkstock; 7 Library of Congress; 8 Library of Congress; 9 Library of Congress; 10 National Archives; 11 Library of Congress; 12 Library of Congress; 13 Thinkstock.

ISBN-13: 978-0-328-67607-1
ISBN-10:   0-328-67607-1

12   17

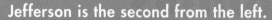
Jefferson is the second from the left.

Do you know which United States president is famous for writing the **Declaration** of **Independence**? Here are some hints. His face is on the nickel and he is one of the presidents carved into Mount Rushmore. He was an architect, a scientist, a farmer, an inventor, and a gifted writer. He is remembered for the words he wrote that helped form a new **government** founded on the rights of the people.

Who is he? He is Thomas Jefferson, our third president.

Early Years

Thomas Jefferson was born in Virginia on April 13, 1743. His family was wealthy, and he grew up on one of his family's large farms.

Education was very important to the Jefferson family, and Jefferson was a gifted student. He was a tall, freckled redhead of 16 when he went off to college. There he met the important people of the South. He studied languages and, soon after, began to study law.

Jefferson was thoughtful and curious. He was also so shy that he did not enjoy speaking in front of others. In fact, Jefferson preferred to express his ideas through his writing. It did not take long for people to notice his skill as a writer.

Jefferson went to William and Mary College in Virginia.

The Rights of the People

Soon after becoming a lawyer, Jefferson was elected to the Virginia **legislature**. Wherever Jefferson went, he made a point of listening carefully when people expressed their views about British rule.

At this time, Great Britain ruled the thirteen **colonies**. The British king and Parliament made the laws that the colonists had to obey. They also set the taxes the colonists had to pay.

Some colonists spoke very openly about their dislike for these laws and taxes. They insisted that the colonies should govern themselves. Jefferson agreed.

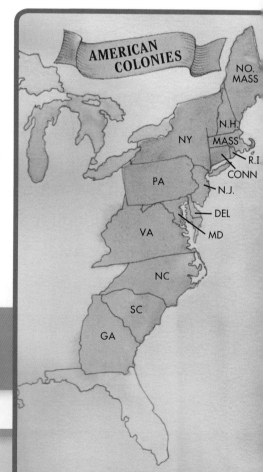

Virginia was one of the thirteen original colonies.

Monticello

Family Life at Monticello

Jefferson was a man of many talents. He spoke several languages, and he played the violin. Not only was he fascinated with the science behind farming, he was also a talented inventor. He is remembered for playful inventions, such as a revolving bookstand.

Jefferson was also a skilled architect. He began to design and build a home on land his father had left to him. He called it Monticello and continued to work on it throughout his life.

In 1772, Jefferson met Martha Skelton, and they married on New Year's Day. They raised their children at Monticello.

Revolution

Like other colonists, Jefferson disliked British rule. He often wrote public papers about his beliefs. Great Britain, he said, did not have the right to rule the colonies.

The colonists grew angrier. Tired of having to obey British laws and tired of paying its taxes, they began to take action. On December 16, 1773, they dumped tea from Great Britain into the Boston Harbor as a sign of protest.

The colonists protested by throwing British tea into the Boston Harbor.

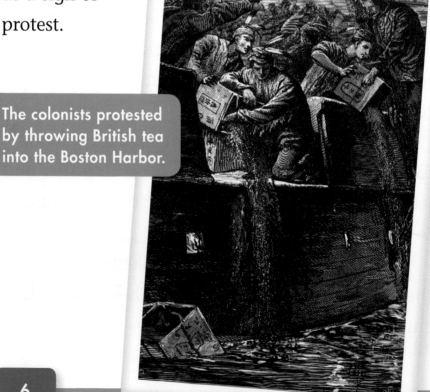

The Declaration

The British government became furious and tightened the freedoms of the colonies. Jefferson responded by writing a booklet in which he stated that the colonies had rights.

In 1774, **representatives** from the colonies came together in Philadelphia for the First Continental Congress. It was time, this Congress said, to discuss what the colonies should do.

Later, Jefferson was elected to the Second Continental Congress. When the Congress decided to declare freedom from Britain, it asked Jefferson to write the Declaration of Independence.

The Continental Congress met in Philadelphia.

Jefferson worked tirelessly on drafting the Declaration of Independence.

With help from Benjamin Franklin and John Adams, Jefferson completed his work in just two weeks.

This Declaration of Independence was a powerful blend of ideas. It clearly stated the complaints the colonies had against the king. It said that people had rights that could not be taken away. "All men are created equal," it proclaimed. Jefferson's words were powerful and inspiring. They still inspire people today.

Return to Virginia

On July 4, 1776, Congress read and signed the Declaration of Independence. The Revolutionary War, the war for independence, had already begun and would last for eight years.

With his work done, Jefferson returned to Virginia. There, he wrote the *Virginia Statute for Religious Freedom* that protected people's right to practice the religion of their own choosing. Jefferson strongly believed in this right. In 1779, Jefferson became the governor of Virginia and served for three years.

After the Declaration of Independence was signed on July 4, 1776, Jefferson returned home to Virginia.

Seven years after Jefferson wrote the Declaration of Independence, the colonies were finally free.

Home in Monticello

When Jefferson retired from public office in Virginia, he returned to Monticello. It was a sad and joyous time. In the fall of 1782, Jefferson's wife died after giving birth to their sixth child. Jefferson was stricken with grief. He spent months at Monticello alone with his children.

Then, in 1783, Jefferson received wonderful news. The United States signed a peace agreement with Great Britain. At long last, America had won its independence.

A New Country

The United States was a brand new country. Many people, including Jefferson, agreed to help form its government. Jefferson was elected to represent Virginia in Congress and brought with him many ideas for the new nation.

One idea involved the land west of the colonies. Jefferson's vision was that the United States should grow in size. He thought this land should become part of the United States.

Jefferson also wanted the United States to have its own money. After all, why should this new country still use England's money? Jefferson's suggestion of a dollar worth a 100 cents was accepted.

Jefferson believed that someday the lands west of the original thirteen states would be valuable to the new country.

Representing the United States

Congress wanted Jefferson to represent the new country in France. While Jefferson was in France, the United States **Constitution** was being written. Jefferson wrote a letter to Congress suggesting that a bill of rights was also needed. When the Bill of Rights was written, it included freedom of the press and freedom of religion. These ideas about basic rights were important to Jefferson.

Newly elected President George Washington then asked Jefferson to return home. He wanted him to become the country's first secretary of state.

President George Washington turned to Thomas Jefferson to be the first secretary of state.

President of the United States

Jefferson was eager to further serve his country. In 1796, he ran for president against John Adams and came in second. The election results meant that Jefferson became the country's second vice president.

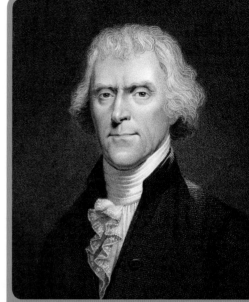

Thomas Jefferson as President

During his presidency, Adams passed laws that banned people from expressing opinions about the government. Jefferson felt this was unacceptable.

As a result, Jefferson decided to run again. This time he won. In 1801, Jefferson became the third president of the United States. The man who had written the Declaration of Independence was now ready to help lead the country.

1743
Jefferson is born
in Virginia.

1779
Jefferson writes Virginia
Statute for Religious Freedom.

1776
Jefferson writes Declaration
of Independence.

1790
Jefferson becomes the
first secretary of state.

The Louisiana Purchase

As president, Jefferson looked to the land that
stretched from west of the Mississippi River to the
Rocky Mountains. Jefferson knew that someday
it would be valuable to the country. In 1803,
Jefferson succeeded in buying the land from
France for fifteen million dollars. The Louisiana
Purchase proved to be one of Jefferson's great
accomplishments. He had doubled the size of the
country without going to war!

Jefferson chose Meriwether Lewis and William
Clark to explore this new land. They returned after
two years with magnificent drawings and useful
information about what they had seen.

1801
Jefferson becomes the third U.S. president.

1825
University of Virginia opens.

1803
Louisiana Purchase doubles size of country.

1826
Jefferson dies on July 4.

Retirement at Monticello

After serving two terms as President, Jefferson returned to his home in Monticello. There he explored his many interests. He wrote letters, collected books, and designed buildings.

One of Jefferson's goals was to provide free education for the people. Not only did he found the University of Virginia, but he designed its buildings as well.

Thomas Jefferson died on July 4, 1826. Remarkably, this was *exactly* fifty years after the Declaration of Independence was signed.

Americans also remember Jefferson for other reasons. His words and ideas helped shape our government and our country.

Glossary

colonies settlements that belong to different countries

Constitution written plan for the United States government

declaration a formal and public statement

government the leaders who run a country and the laws that the people in the country follow

independence freedom, liberty

legislature a group of people who have the authority to make laws

representative a person chosen to speak for a larger group